DRY IT
⌐YOU'LL LIKE IT!

A BOOK ABOUT FOOD DEHYDRATION

BY GEN MacMANIMAN

FALL CITY, WASHINGTON 98024
U.S.A.

DRY IT~ YOU'LL LIKE IT!

is available through the publisher:

MacManiman Inc

~ Living Foods Dehydrator ~

P.O. Box 546 ~ 3023 362nd SE

Fall City, Washington · 98024

1973 ~ First Printing
1983 ~ Revised Edition
1997 ~ 27th Printing
(270,000 copies in print!)

Printed in the U.S.A.
Evergreen Printing Co.
Seattle, Washington

This book is brought to you with love from

Paula B. Calderón
Printing, artwork, & compilation

Bob MacManiman
Designer, Living Foods Dehydrator

Gen MacManiman
"Seed Woman"

Betty Rae Green
Plans & construction details

CONTENTS

"AFTERTHOUGHTS"

LIVING FOODS DEHYDRATOR

WHY DRY?

We know why <u>we</u> like to dry foods! And depending on our mood, any of the following reasons could come first:

IT IS A FIRST-CLASS WAY TO PRESERVE FOOD:
It's cheap & it's easy. Properly-dried food (un-cooked, dried quickly at low temperatures) is nutritionally superior to canned food — & no pre-servatives or other chemicals are required. The on-going electrical drain of a freezer is eliminated. Flavor & appetizing color are maintained. <u>One-sixth or less</u> of the usual storage space is required. Carefully-stored dried foods will keep for several seasons.

DRIED FOOD MEANS INSTANT, TASTY NUTRITION FOR PEOPLE ON THE GO.
Whether "on the go" means lunch on the run dur-ing a day full of errands, or a quick meal on the trail with several miles to cover before dark, or a stand-up snack before vacuming the living room —— busy people need <u>real food.</u> Dried fruits, whole-grain wafers, a cup of broth made from dried, powdered vegetables from your own garden — these are real food! Not just empty calories, but good-tasting, life-sustaining food.

THE VARIETY OF FOODS WHICH CAN BE PRESERVED
BY DRYING IS ENORMOUS. (Just page through
this book!)

Fruits & berries make delicious, quick-energy eating ; vegetables go into broth, soups & casseroles,
& may be powdered & used for seasoning; herbs
brew into delicate, healthful teas, & season many
dishes ; meat & fish jerky are good anytime, especially when hiking or camping; breads & cereals
take the form of crunchy wafers, granola, & whole-
grain cookies; confections of fruit, nuts, grains &
honey delight your tastebuds and your body.

NOTHING IS WASTED when you have a dehydrator
& use it — from small amounts of produce that
might ordinarily decompose in a corner of the refrigerator, to an over-abundant zucchini crop.
Almost everything can be dried & used to add
nutrition to future meals.   And don't forget —
it's a year-round activity!   With herbs in the
spring, berries, fruits & vegetables in the summer
& fall, bananas & grains in the winter, our dehydrator is as busy as we want it to be.

We continue to be amazed at the opportunities for
creativity in the field of food dehydration. A glance
at the recipes in this book will give you the idea...
May you have as much fun & good eating as we do!

GETTING STARTED

This book is for anyone who wants to dehydrate food. There are plans at the end of the book for a well-designed, functional dehydrator which you may eventually want to build. But if a small-scale beginning is more to your taste, here are some ideas:

An area with a fairly constant temperature of 95°—100° is required. To help to locate the spot, a fish tank thermometer (range of 85°—120°) is useful. Consider these possibilities:
. . . top of the refrigerator
. . . near a hot-water heater (we built a small rack over ours)
. . . near a furnace
. . . over a heat register, electric heater or radiator
. . . an oven with a pilot light (ovens usually are less than ideal — too hot & not enough air movement)
. . . a rack suspended over a wood range

You may think of others. Remember that ▶ air flow is almost as important as heat for proper drying, & darkness, though not mandatory, is preferred (particularly for herbs). Avoid dusty areas, or devise a protective covering for your rack.

An efficient drying rack can easily be fashioned from hardware cloth, a very stiff metal mesh. Two sides may be bent down to form "legs" if they are required. However, we suggest covering the hardware cloth with food-safe screen material, to prevent the food from coming into direct contact with metal.   Or use cooking parchment or plastic wrap, as described in the General Instructions.

These ideas should give a good start; once you've begun, you'll think of more.   It won't be long before your small-scale beginning increases its proportions.

Foods dried quickly at a temperature of (usually) no more than 110° have their life-force intact.   They are vital & life-sustaining.   No chemicals or additives are involved — they simply are not needed.   And one could hardly ask for better "shelf life!"   Properly packaged & stored, dried foods will keep for several seasons, & in minimal space.   They are delicious & versatile.

We have learned a lot, since we began, & most of it by trial-&-error.   Let us share with you the high points, so that you may avoid some obvious pitfalls & continue in your own creative fashion — sharing, we hope, your discoveries with us.

GENERAL INSTRUCTIONS

Remember that ▶MOVEMENT OF WARM AIR is the principle of this dehydrator. Conditions at all times should encourage this movement of air. Foods & herbs should be arranged with open spaces between pieces to expedite drying. (After the original wilting or shrinking, materials can be con~ solidated to make more room available.)
▶ Loosely arranged material is the rule of thumb!

TEMPERATURE control requires the use of a thermometer to help the operator become familiar with management of various materials to be dried. Temperatures should range between 95° & 105° — not more* than 110°.
▶ The warmer temperatures require closer supervision so that drying may be stopped at the ideal point.
Temperature is controlled first by proper regulation of the heating unit, & second, by

VENTILATION. The top cover of your dehydrator is more than it may seem! It provides both work

〜〜〜〜〜〜〜

* We want to preserve the whole food — color & flavor, yes; but complete with vitamins, minerals & enzymes.

surface & ventilation control, vital to proper dehy~
dration. Top must be open (pulled forward) to
allow for removal of moisture from drying foods,
& to help control temperature. Amount of opening
will vary, but usually about TWO INCHES is ample.
(Top should be closed when unit is not in use, to
keep interior dust-free.)
The dryer top is designed to be a functional work
surface, for preparation & packaging of dried
materials. The addition of a small cutting board
will help to keep the top smooth & easy to clean.

TRAY CARE is simple & easy. Wiping with a damp
cloth is often all that is needed. When necessary,
trays can be washed & brushed in a bathtub (or out~
side, with a hose), towel-dried & replaced in the
dehydrator to dry.
► Don't overload your trays! They'll hold a lot,
but too much weight will cause stretching. The
heavy-duty, hardware-cloth tray is designed for
weightier items. Reasonable care in handling will
assure a long life for the trays.

LOAD LIMITS, ETC. . . . If operation instructions
have been followed, the dehydrator should work at
full capacity. However, if, for instance, all trays are
filled with moist fruit the drying may seem slow
at first ——— but temperature checking & tray

rotation will assure that dehydration proceeds successfully.   Tray rotation simply means to keep the
food nearest completion on the bottom, so that
moisture from other trays won't be transferred
to the nearly-dry material.   (Remember that
heat, & moisture with it, rises.)   Turning trays
a quarter-turn each time you check the contents
of your dryer, will also help ensure even drying.

DRYING VERY JUICY FOODS (fruit leathers,
etc.) is easy with the help of a plastic wrap like
Saran or Handi-Wrap.   12" x 18" is the approximate size to use on each tray.   Fastening the
edges here & there with masking tape helps
to prevent their curling over the drying food.
Parchment paper, such as that used by bakeries,
is excellent for "baking" Granola (& Breakfast
Cookies~ see the recipes!).
▶   There is a best method for using either
plastic wrap or parchment paper for efficient
dehydration: using the 12" x 18" pieces, place
the plastic on the extreme right or left half of
the tray, alternating sides with each successive
tray (ie., right half of bottom tray, left half
of next higher tray, etc.).   This will create a
back & forth air flow for faster dehydration.
Remember ~ although you may carefully space
food on top of the paper, the paper itself will

block air flow ⌇ so don't cover much more than one-half of the tray with the paper or plastic.

ALWAYS LEAVE SPACE ON A TRAY OF DRYING FOOD FOR AIR FLOW! THIS IS ESSENTIAL!

STRONG - SMELLING FOODS, such as fish, should be dried separately, but may be placed directly on trays.
Wash trays after such use to be sure that any odor or residue will not affect the flavor of whatever is dried next.

▶ CAREFUL STORAGE is vital for keeping foods at peak quality. Correct storage must eliminate moisture, air & light, & at the same time remain convenient. For this purpose, fairly heavy plastic bags are both functional & reuseable.
Store ▶ small quantities of everything ⌇ an amount suitable for your own family's needs. This not only makes it simpler for you to use your stored food, but also prevents contamination of large amounts of food should a small quantity, for any reason, begin to spoil.   [This is real food ⌇ no added colors, no chemical preservatives ⌇ & it can be mighty tempting to a bug! Careful storage will prevent possible insect infestation.]

Putting the food or herb into a small brown _paper_ _bag_ is an ideal first step: the paper both shuts out light & prevents long-term contact of food with plastic, avoiding possible interaction. Fold the bag snugly about the food, then put it into a _plastic bag_ of similar size. Tightly fasten the plastic bag with a twist tab, or fold top down & seal with masking tape. Several small packages may then be put into a _large_ plastic bag, to be sealed in similar fashion. For long-term storage, this bag should go into a _third_ plastic bag, to make three fairly heavy layers of plastic to protect the food; or a large air-tight container would do a good job.

Glass containers are excellent, too, but they do require more shelf room. Careful consideration must be taken to seal jars securely, so that no air or moisture can enter. With all the stored foods, & especially your herbs, ▶ _darkness_ is vital.

Storing fruit leathers is simple enough...roll your leather first in waxed butcher paper, then put it into plastic bags as required.

Short-term storage, obviously, is less critical & allows for some modification of the rules... No need for three layers of protection if you plan to munch it up within the week!

If at any time an opened package of dehydrated food is less crisp than desired, it can easily be re-crisped in the dehydrator. (This is important when grinding herbs & vegetables into powder... They must be <u>completely</u> dry.)

LABEL EVERYTHING!

Labeling is part of packaging. It is quite disconcerting to pick up a lovely package of herb tea & wonder just what it is! (When drying several kinds at once, this can happen within <u>minutes</u> of bagging it.) In the herb kingdom there are many look-alikes and even smell-alikes.

▶ The correct <u>name</u> <u>and</u> <u>date</u>, on every package, should be apparent at a glance.

MORE ON PLASTIC AND PARCHMENT.

Plastic wrap is necessary for drying the "soupier" foods, like fruit leather purées, which cannot be placed directly on the screens. Different brands give different results, some not so desirable. Experiment with several.

Parchment paper, suggested for drying granola & breakfast cookies, may not be readily available. For granola, butcher paper works fine. Cookies may also be placed ➤ directly on the screens.

Where better to begin?

APPLES

Apples are the most versatile of all fruits (Johnny Appleseed knew!) Dried apples are no different. . .

APPLES ⌇ You can slice 'em, dice 'em, chunk 'em, leather 'em & combine 'em ⌇ with other fruits, with seeds, nuts & grains. They make a binder for dried wafers & confections.

Dry them SLICED, DICED, CHUNKED, even SHREDDED.
▶ ¼-inch slices are about right. (Keep pieces close to the same size for even drying.) With diced & chunked apples, the smaller pieces dry faster & quality is preserved. Dry everything ⌇ even peels & trimmings.
▶ Approximate drying time is about two days.

To use dried apples for a mild, good-tasting juice; just soak apple parts in water (this is where you may use the trimmings.)
A thin slice of apple dried crisp makes delicious munching. To soften for eating out-of-hand, pour a little water over fruit, drain & let set a few hours in a covered jar. Or simply leave the package open a day or two & let the moisture in the air soften the apples.

☆ APPLE LEATHER (PLAIN)
(This is a _basic_ _recipe_.)

. . . a "scroll" of dried puréed fruit. Chewy, delicious, &
so simple!

Prepare about _one_ _quart_ chopped apples, removing cores
but not skins.   Place just enough water in the blender,
with a few apple chunks, to start the blending action . . .
keep adding apples until consistency is that of good
apple sauce.

▶ Prepare plastic wrap: about 12" x 18," held down to
tray with a bit of masking tape, to prevent curling.
Spread apple purée evenly onto plastic (about ¼"
thick — it gets thinner as it dries).

▶ Approximate drying time: about two days.

VARIATIONS!   (This is the fun part)

"APPLE BUTTER" LEATHER
. . . to the blended apples add:
   2 Tbsp. cider vinegar or lemon juice
   2 tsp. mixed spices (such as pumpkin pie spice, or
           your own blend — coriander, nutmeg, etc.)
  ¼ cup honey, or to taste
Continue as in basic leather.

APPLE-RAISIN (or DATE) LEATHER

. . . soak one cup raisins (or chopped dates) until soft, in water to cover. Blend with the soaking liquid, adding apple chunks until consistency is like thick applesauce.

. . . Proceed as for plain leather.

APPLE-FRUIT COMBINATION LEATHERS

. . . Start with a one-to-one ratio; adjust to your own taste. . . Try blending apples with pitted prunes, dates, plums, peaches, apricots; with bananas. . . berries . . . Try them all!

IF IT TASTES GOOD IN THE BLENDER, IT WILL TASTE GOOD AS A LEATHER!

▶ Blend juicier fruits first, & no water will be needed to start apples blending (for instance, bananas require no water to blend).

. . . You may wish to blend "seedy" berries alone, then strain & return to blender before adding apples. But remember that seeds are an excellent, concentrated food!

In the making, all of these leathers are delicious sauces, and you may wish to enjoy them that way. Sprinkle a few ground nuts on top for a beautiful raw breakfast.

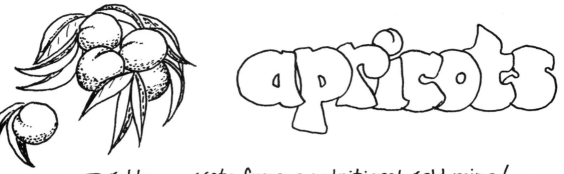

apricots

golden nuggets from a nutritional gold mine!

DRIED, the apricot becomes a year-round delicious fruit, well worth what it may cost in money & effort . . . organic & tree-ripened, of course!

TO DRY . . .
Small pieces dry faster & the finished fruit retains its color & flavor.   So ▶ cut small ⌒ halve the halves, & sometimes even halve the quarters.
▶   APRICOTS need to be quite dry to KEEP. Dry until quite hard & completely moisture-free. STORE in small plastic bags inside of larger ones (several small bags of fruit inside one big one make any amount you wish available easily).   Even then, it is well to store inside an airtight container. CORRECT STORAGE IS SO IMPORTANT!

TO USE THE DRIED FRUIT . . . soften overnight in water to cover.   Enjoy as is, or use the softened fruit & liquid to make leathers or binder for wafers, etc.

APRICOT LEATHER

. . . So chewy & flavorful with nothing added; the taste is a sweet/tart combination hard to beat!

▶ If the fruit is ripe & soft, the pitted halves will blend with no added liquid. The rule-of-thumb is to begin with enough fruit to get the blender action started; then add a few pieces at a time (blending continuously) until blender capacity is reached.

Pour the purée onto prepared plastic wrap (see General Instructions), smoothing with spatula or jiggling tray until about ¼" thick ⟶ it always varies slightly. If you have a large amount of purée, make more than one leather.

▶ The thicker the leather, the chewier it will be, & the longer the drying time. Thin leathers will dry in less than 24 hours.

∽VARIATIONS∿

. . . honey to sweeten, to taste

. . . combined half & half with apples (add coriander)

. . . add one cup chopped dates to blended apricots

. . . half & half with raspberries (strain out seeds); add honey (this may dry a bit sticky, but we promise no one will mind!)

▶ Apricot purée makes a perfect binder for confections.

bananas

So sweet & versatile! Stalk the markets for bar~
gains of ripe & "overripe" bananas . . . when natural
ripening has transformed hard-to-digest starch
into sweet, natural sugar. Banana bargains often
occur in winter ~ keep you & your dryer busy
when local fruit is not available.

DRY WHEN THE BANANAS ARE BEAUTIFULLY SPOTTED WITH BROWN!

There are several methods :

1. Slice directly onto tray (no overlapping) & let
   dry completely before removing. They may
   appear to stick, but when dry are easily removed.
   This method gives excellent color to the finished
   product.
2. Dry peeled, whole bananas for a day; then stack
   several at once for mass slicing. This method
   seems to give chewier consistency to banana bits.
3. "Banana sticks" are made by quartering a half-
   banana the long way . . .
   These pieces dry fastest
   of all, & do not stick
   when laid on tray with cut side up.
   Fun to eat!

≋ BANANA LEATHER ≋

Absolutely no need ever to waste another banana!

▶ Blend your <u>very</u> ripe bananas (those soft, brown-skinned ones) in blender with no added liquid. A wedge of organic lemon (with peel) will give a special flavor.
Pour onto plastic wrap & spread thin... that's all!
Dries in less than 12 hours.

Banana leathers lend themselves to some luxurious <u>VARIATIONS</u>... Try these (for a start!):
...Throw in a handful of walnuts at the very <u>end</u> of the blending, so they'll be chunky, not pulverized.
...Combine with any tart fruit ⌒ apples, apricots.
...Play with spices & flavorings ⌒ vanilla, coriander...

Roll this one over your tongue!
BANANANUT FREEZECREME

Soak ▶ 4 oz. <u>dried bananas</u> in enough water to make 1½ cups of bananas & liquid
Blend soaked bananas & add ¼ cup oil, 1 tsp. vanilla, & ¼ cup honey... blend in thoroughly. Add 1 cup walnuts & blend briefly (so nuts will still be chunky).
Serve as is, or ▶ <u>soft-freeze</u>, for a most surprising, delicious, creamy, marshmallowy dessert!

BERRIES*

*all kinds — plus GRAPES & CURRANTS

IN GENERAL (READ THIS; IT'S IMPORTANT):

Berries are usually so juicy you'll use them in ways slightly different from other fruits. They're excellent for "spiking" leathers — especially apple, which has enough natural pectin to compensate for the extra juiciness.

▶ When making an all-berry leather, it's best to add pectin (or you might experiment with ground flax seed or other meal for thickening). SEE "Grape 'Jam' Leather" in this section.

The following ideas should get you off to a fine start . . . As for flavor combinations, your own tongue is of course the very best judge. Remember the rule: ▶ If it tastes good in your blender, it will taste good as a leather!

APPLE - BERRY LEATHER

Apples are great with virtually any berry. For directions, please refer to "Apple- Fruit Combination Leathers," in the APPLE section. If apples &/or berries are quite tart, add honey to taste.

BANANA - BERRY LEATHER

Yum! Banana - blackberry, banana - raspberry, whatever. You may wish to blend berries first,

then sieve to remove seeds. Return berries to
blender & add bananas. (One-to-one is a good
banana-berry ratio, but it may easily be varied.)
Continue as in basic Apple Leather.

<u>PLEASE NOTE</u>: Because of their sweet juiciness,
some of the berry leathers will dry somewhat "tacky."
(Don't let that deter you!) These leathers are
probably best not kept for extended periods.

TO SIMPLY DRY BERRIES:
Dry whole, freshly-picked berries by spreading
over 12 x 18" plastic wrap (refer to GENERAL IN-
STRUCTIONS)... <u>Handle</u> <u>carefully</u>, so they don't
"bleed" & lose precious juice. They will dry quite
hard.
A good way to use the thoroughly-dried berries
is to grind them fine in a seed grinder & pour
a small amount of hot water over, allowing them
to steep.   Sweeten with honey & enjoy as jam or
topping for fruit salad, whatever . . . may be combined with other fruit for a wintertime leather.

CURRANTS
Dry as above, basically to use in place of raisins
where desired. They are less sweet, but very
nice in mixed-fruit recipes.

CHERRIES

...May be dried with or without the pits...(they do dry faster with pits removed). If very juicy after pitting, place on parchment paper or plastic wrap for the initial drying.

We can't wait to try CHERRY LEATHER!

CRANBERRIES

May be dried to soak later for refreshing JUICE.

CRANBERRY LEATHER is unexpectedly delicious.

Use dates to sweeten the tart berries:

Soak one cup of pitted, chopped dates in water to cover, until soft. Blend dates & liquid 'til quite smooth, then add about one cup of cranberries. Blend again; continue as in basic Apple Leather.

CRANBERRY - FRUIT CHEWS ～ Something special!

Blend 2 small apples with water as required, as in basic Apple Leather. Add ½# very ripe cranberries, blending 'til smooth. Add about 1 cup pitted, chopped dates, blending only briefly so dates will be chunky. Stir in 1 cup chopped walnuts. Add honey to taste. Smooth this mixture onto plastic wrap (SEE "Very Juicy Foods" in the General Instructions) ～ Make it very thick, about ½". Dry until firm enough to cut into squares ～ they will be delightfully chewy. Do not overdry!

GRAPES

Dry any good seedless grapes, until the "feel" is right, for RAISINS.

GRAPE LEATHER

Combine pulp from Concord grapes with apple & honey to make leather. (SEE "Apple-Fruit Combination Leathers.")

GRAPE "JAM" LEATHER

Blend one quart Concord grapes with one package powdered pectin & ½ cup or more honey. Proceed as with basic Apple Leather.

▶ <u>DON'T FORGET</u> to note <u>your</u> favorite combinations:

PEACHES . . .

TO DRY PEACHES:

<u>Wash</u> & <u>defuzz</u> with a terry towel
(peeling is not necessary).   Then cut
¼" slices directly onto the tray. They may seem
too juicy, but try it anyway. . . As they dry,
the slices stick to the tray, but when completely
dry they remove very easily, & retain their great
looks.

<u>To use</u>. . . No instructions needed! Just eat &
enjoy, although if desired the fruit may be soaked
& eaten with cream & a little honey.

PEACH LEATHER

Blend ripe, pitted peaches. . . sweeten with a bit
of honey if desired.   Add a touch of spice if you
like; perhaps ground coriander.   Continue as in
basic Apple Leather.

The delicate peach flavor is delicious alone, but
apples combine with it beautifully, & give the
leather a fine consistency with their natural
pectin. (Blend the juicy peaches first ⟶ no
water necessary ⟶ adding apple chunks to the
purée & continuing to blend.   This avoids the
need for any extra liquid.)   Tuck it away for
winter if you can hide it fast enough!

...& PEARS

TO DRY PEARS:

Once again, <u>small pieces</u> are the rule of thumb.
Quarter the washed fruit ⁓ DO NOT PEEL ⁓
& then slice thin, for <u>fast drying</u> assures a quality
product.   (This does <u>not</u> mean accelerated heat.
Keep the temperature, as usual, around 100°.)
It is unnecessary even to core pears, since the
whole fruit is deliciously edible when dried. You
will find your delicate-hued, beautifully-translucent
dried pears to be an aesthetic pleasure as well!

PEAR LEATHER

Nothing need be added to pears for leather; perhaps a touch of spice if desired.   Follow
instructions for Apple Leather... pour, dry, & enjoy!

plums, prunes

Home-dehydrated prunes excel in every way... so little value is lost. The juice of the soaked, reconstituted fruit is even red instead of the brown of commercial prunes.

▶ FAST DRYING (small pieces) is the secret! Pit the plums or prunes & quarter them... cut even smaller if fruit is extra-large. Lay on tray with skin-side down. These small pieces will be ready days sooner than if dried whole, & will be of better quality.

For LEATHER, prunes are tart & delicious with nothing added, but for sweetness try adding dates or raisins or honey. Prunes combine nicely with apples in leathers. (SEE Apple-Fruit Combination Leathers, for how-to.)

Often a juicy fruit such as prunes will need thickening to make a good leather. You may use about one Tbsp. ground flax seed for each cup blended fruit, for a simple thickening. Flax does not change the fruit taste, except perhaps to mellow tartness. It does seem to give a good texture, & of course it increases nutritional value.

pineapple

There is really no way to describe the taste of a tidbit of dried pineapple! Be warned that after you have sampled this chewy, indescribably sweet bit of concentrated sunlight & fruit sugar, you'll almost certainly lose any craving for artificial sweets. We believe our pineapple tidbits are an aid to the digestion, so enzyme-rich is this wonderful fruit ~ we often enjoy some after a meal.

▶ Watch for bargain days & select several pineapples: when golden, slightly soft & fragrant, the fruit will be sweetest.
Wash, even scrub the outside, then quarter the long way. This gives you a pineapple "boat," to assist you in drying this very juicy fruit. Chunk the pineapple by making parallel slices in both directions (don't cut the peel), then slice under the still-attached chunks, next to the peel. With practice, all the pieces will remain intact on the "boat." Now, set the fruit-on-a-boat onto a piece of parchment paper to begin drying.
▶ These will be heavier than most fruit, so don't overload your trays. When the chunks are less juicy, empty them off their boats to finish drying on parchment or plastic wrap.
And here's what you do with the "boats"...

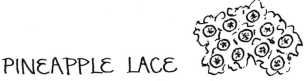

PINEAPPLE LACE

Scrape the pulp from the pineapple rind onto a piece of plastic wrap (see the "Juicy Fruits" section of the General Instructions). Spread it to a scant ½" thickness (it gets thin as it dries). Carefully lay banana slices onto the pineapple so that they barely touch each other... as they dry they will shrink.

When it dries, you will have a beautiful fruit "lace" ... Hold it up to the light to fully appreciate it, before biting in!

Bet you haven't thought of this before!

RHUBARB

Tart, dried rhubarb is surprisingly thirst-quenching, & couldn't be easier:

Slice rhubarb into ¼" pieces & dry — that's all!

Although it's nice to nibble dried rhubarb, the following recipe is our favorite way to use it:

RHUBARB-ADE

Throw a handful or two of dried rhubarb into a jug of fresh cool water & let it juice for one or two hours. Sweeten with honey if you like.

Makes a delicious, refreshing drink. Add to punches!

Here are a couple of nice ways to use your dried fruit:

FRUIT COMPOTE

Soak the following dried fruits together, in any amounts you wish, for several hours or overnight:

chopped prunes   peaches

pears   raisins

apricots   chopped dates

(water to cover)

Add chopped dates & sunflower seeds for the last hour or so of soaking.

Makes an especially satisfying breakfast ⁓ a delicious dessert.

FRUIT TIDBITS

Soak chopped, dried fruits, in water to cover:

prunes   raisins   (vary amount of each,

peaches   dates   for different flavor

apricots   etc.   combinations)

To about 2 cups of soaked fruit, stir in about 1 cup chopped nuts.

Blend apricots or apple chunks as for leather, & add 1½ cups of the purée to the fruit/nut mixture. Spread about ½" thick onto tray prepared with plastic wrap (see General Instructions: "Juicy Fruits"). Dry until surface is dry & fruit feels firm ... turn it over onto tray, removing plastic, & continue drying until the exposed side is also dry & firm. Cut into squares & return to dehydrator for a little more drying.

vegetables

The real joy of owning & using a dehydrator becomes evident when you realize that virtually nothing from your garden need ever be wasted again. Every little handful of extras can be dried & saved, complete with vitamins, minerals & enzymes ⌐ not to mention their appetizing color! We have dehydrated nearly everything we grow, with many interesting results.

HOW TO USE DRIED VEGETABLES

This whole activity of food dehydration revolves, for us, around the need to preserve the real value of every bit of food. So we are learning to use our wonderful vegetables in their raw state . . . what isn't used fresh from the garden is dried, to be munched later out-of-hand, or powdered in the seed mill. These powdered vegetables add flavor & nutrition to our broths, raw soups, salads, dressings . . . Without a doubt there is many a dish which may be enhanced by such an addition. Some sliced, dried vegetables, like zucchini, make lovely "chips" for dipping.

As for additional uses or recipes, we will mostly leave you to your own adventuring. Herewith, some drying information:

VEGETABLES WE HAVE DRIED (so far)

beets	garlic	parsley
cabbage	green beans	parsnip
cabbage blossoms	horseradish	snow peas
carrots & tops	kolrabi	squash
chard	leek	tomatoes
corn	mustard greens	turnips
cucumbers	onion	zucchini

This list is not intended to limit you! Rather, see in it the almost endless possibilities open to you & your dryer.

The following paragraphs contain some methods for drying & tips for using a few specific vegetables. Please remember, ► drying techniques are generally applicable . . . so review your General Instructions. ► Specific hints are listed under the foods to which they apply & of course fit any similar food as well.

ALL LEAFY VEGETABLES
Arrange clean leaves loosely on trays to allow adequate air flow. Drying materials may be consolidated as they shrink, making room for more (keep the new, moister materials on upper trays, as explained in General Instructions). Dry until the leaves crumble when handled & all moisture is gone.

FOR HOW-TO-STORE, SEE GENERAL INSTRUCTIONS.

VEGETABLES

CORN
Husked sweet corn can be dried right on the cob.
Remember — they'll be a bit heavy, so don't overload
trays.   When thoroughly dry, the
kernels come right off in the hands:
hold an end of the cob in one hand,
then grasp & twist the free end with
your other hand.   The small black
Indian corn is especially adaptable to
raw-eating.   When soaked, it is sweet
& delicious in salads, soups.   Corn
silk is not only useful as an herb, but when dried &
powdered can add a nice "corny" flavor to a soup.
Don't forget the dried <u>corn</u> <u>chip</u> recipe! (See GRAINS.)

GREEN BEANS
Choose tender, young beans & cut as desired, either
strips (which dry fastest) or slices.   Dried beans
powder nicely in a seed mill for adding to broth, etc.

ONION, LEEK & GARLIC
The lovely green tops, dried & powdered, are mild &
delicious . . . a very condiment especially fine in
salad dressings. The bulbs, sliced & dried, will save
the day when no fresh ones are available.
When drying, ▶ use parchment to keep that strong
flavor from direct contact with the trays.

TOMATOES

Cut into small wedges & let each rest on its skin-side to dry. This keeps the juice in so flavor & nutrition are enhanced. Fascinating to chew & a great flavor addition to broths, etc.

ZUCCHINI OR CUCUMBER CHIPS

Slice fairly thin (scant ¼") —— or to personal preference (experiment a little! But try to keep each batch the same size, for even drying). Dry until crisp & use with chip dips ——your own, freshly-made, of course. Truly great nibbling!

BLOSSOMS ARE FOOD, TOO!

Blossoms from the garden which land in our salads have included cabbage, parsley, celery & radish flowers. Violets & wild pansies make delicious & beautiful salad fare . . . Loveliest fresh, of course, but the dried blooms add their subtle nutrients to wintertime salads, too.

Remember to use QUALITY VEGETABLES . . . the end result can't be better than what you start with, so always start with the best!

VEGETABLE BROTH MIX

. . . to be kept on hand for delicious quick energy (pour boiling water over & let steep a minute). Also makes a great seasoning for other dishes.

Suggested ingredients:
cabbage, carrots, celery (any part), garlic, green beans, horseradish, mushrooms, mustard greens, onion, parsley, peas & pods, peppers, spinach, tomato, watercress, & anything else you think of.

▶ Powder your ingredients & combine as you please. If the right flavor combination eludes you, or you haven't enough ingredients, use any good powdered vegetable broth for a base & add your own "extras."

▶ Broth may be thickened if desired with a spoonful of ground flaxseed. We've also used ground millet, chia, or other seeds, with pleasing results.

▶ Add dried, powdered herbs for even greater nutrition. We use any of a variety — comfrey, nettle, chickweed, malva, plantain, lamb's quarters — any of the edible weeds.

GARLIC BROTH

A fantastic warmer-upper, any time of year:

. . . to a fresh, hot cupful of vegetable broth (facing page), add one clove of garlic, crushed, a dash of soy sauce, & cayenne, or capsicum, to taste. Add a little fresh tomato juice (or if you like, blend your broth with a few chunks of tomato), if you have some.

If you're really <u>hungry</u>, make it in a soup bowl — remember the ground flaxseed, to thicken — & add a big handful of sprouts.   A real meal!

DON'T FORGET <u>MUSHROOMS</u>!

The first step is to try to pick your mushrooms "clean" — cut them off at ground level & brush off loose dirt & leaves. No need to wash them; if you spread them on trays & allow them to dry about a day (until surface is no longer sticky), you can easily brush off any remaining dirt. Trim if necessary. Replace trays & allow the clean mushrooms to dry thoroughly.

► Don't let the initial drying take too long, or the dirt will be firmly embedded as the mushrooms shrivel.

► If your mushrooms have come from the grocery, you'll probably want to wash them before dehydrating. Allow them to drain on a towel before putting into dryer.

seeds, grains

Those wonderful, living grains & seeds! — give them a chance to nourish your wonderful living _body_! With a dehydrator, you'll find there's no need to cook the life out of grains... Delicious uncooked wafers, flatbreads & cookies are all possible with dehydration.

▶ Once you get the "feel" of the recipes which follow, we hope you'll discover there's more than one way to do things. Substitute other grains & seeds; change amounts. We like these recipes, but please don't stop with them! They are just a beginning.

(Some grains & seeds we like to keep on hand:)

Seeds	Grains	Sprouts
chia	barley	alfalfa
flax	millet	lentils
pumpkin	oats	mung
sesame	rice	rice
sunflower	rye	wheat
	sweet corn	other grains
	wheat	

GRANOLA

This is one of our favorite versions. There's probably nothing as adaptable as a granola recipe, so use what you have on hand, & have fun!

Mix together:
   ½ cup honey (or more, to taste)
   ½ cup hot water
   ½ cup oil
   2 tsp. vanilla

Pour it over
   4 to 5 cups oatmeal, in a large bowl
...& allow to soak, while adding (right on top):
   1 cup raw sunflower seeds
   1 cup sesame seeds
   1 cup flax seeds
   1 cup freshly-grated coconut, if you have it
   ¾ cup chopped walnuts
   ¾ cup chopped dates, or raisins or currants

Mix it all together & spread on parchment to dry. To speed drying, spread thinly. Takes about 2 days — longer if more honey or water is used in mixing. Store in plastic bags or jars in refrigerator.

VARIATIONS: Change ingredients &/or amounts as you please. Try adding or substituting chia seeds, fresh wheat germ, almonds, cashews or other nuts, a little brewer's yeast, chopped dried fruit, whatever.

"14-GRAIN" WAFERS

The "14 grains" are as follows:

alfalfa	lentils	rye
barley	millet	sesame
buckwheat	mung beans	wheat
corn	oats	almonds
flax	rice	

Combine in more or less equal amounts & soak as for sprouting. (Sprout if you wish.) Place about a cupful in blender with enough water to blend easily. Add some soaked raisins to sweeten (about ¼ cup) & blend until very smooth. If you have them, add ¼ cup ground chia seeds (these thicken the mixture immediately, improving texture & food value). Spread evenly over parchment (to scant ¼") & allow to dry... remove the paper & continue drying on screen until thoroughly dry, turning once or twice. Cut into squares.

APPLE & SPROUT WAFERS

Blend 2-day sprouted grains ("14-grain" mix, if you like) half-&-half with chopped apples in blender, with enough water to support blending action. Handle as a leather, drying on plastic wrap (see basic Apple Leather). When quite dry, remove the plastic & turn leather to finish drying thoroughly.

AN OCCASIONAL REVIEW OF THE GENERAL INSTRUCTIONS (FRONT OF BOOK) HELPS YOU ACHIEVE PERFECT RESULTS!

CORN CHIPS
(Great with garlic broth!)

<u>Blend until smooth</u>:

   3 cups fresh tomatoes (somewhat chopped)

   1/4 cup or more chopped onion

   3 cloves garlic, crushed (we smash 'em between
               layers of heavy plastic)

   2 Tbsp. oil (mild, cold-pressed)

   1 tsp. each cayenne, dried dill<u>weed</u> (not the
             seed), & sea salt

<u>Mix in bowl</u>:

   3 cups finely ground dried sweet corn (the black
             Indian corn is our favorite)

   1 cup ground flaxseed (for texture — or use all corn)

Mix it all together & spread as thinly as possible on
parchment paper. When it seems quite dry, remove
the paper & dry on screen until very crisp.

CORNAPPLE CRISPS

   1/2 cup ground sweet corn, or black Indian corn

   1 cup blended raw apple sauce (see Basic Apple
             Leather for method)

   1/8 tsp. cayenne

   1/8 tsp. ground rock salt or sea salt

Mix together & spread about 1/4" thick on plastic
wrap. Dry until crisp, as above.

<u>NOTE</u>: Mixtures containing fruit should be dried on
      plastic wrap, to prevent sticking.

CORNAPPLE CHEWS

So great you have to have another to believe it!

Soak overnight:

    1 cup dried sweet corn (we like the sweet black
               Indian corn best), in

    1 cup water

Put soaked corn & water into <u>blender</u>, with

    1 large apple, cored & chopped (with skin)
    ½ cup raisins

<u>Blend</u>, adding water as required to keep blades moving, until quite smooth.

<u>Spread</u> ¼" thick on plastic wrap prepared as described in General Instructions. ► Do not overdry. This is a chewy wafer. You'll <u>know</u> when it's ready!

<u>NOTE</u>: Grain wafers can be varied surprisingly with different techniques. The great texture difference between a Cornapple Crisp & a Cornapple Chew is achieved by grinding the dry sweet corn for one; soaking & then blending that same dried corn for the other. Both are great. Try it with other recipes. Vive la différence!

<u>CUTTING</u> CRISPY CRUNCHY WAFERS can be difficult. We generally just break them into pieces, but if you like squares, cut them while dry enough to hold their shape but not so crisp they'll crumble. Use a cutting board & a sharp knife. Then return the squares to the dryer until crisp as desired.

SESAME~PUMPKINSEED BITS

Another favorite — & too easy <u>not</u> to try!

<u>Stir together</u>:
 ½ cup honey & ¼ cup hot water

<u>Mix in</u>:
 2 cups sesame seeds
 1 cup pumpkinseeds

<u>Spread</u> about ¼" thick over prepared plastic wrap (see General Instructions). Pat gently into place — the mixture will be crumbly.

<u>Score</u> (cut partially into squares). When firm, remove plastic wrap & turn over to continue drying until crisp. Break into squares along scored lines & dry a little more.

VARIATIONS: — use maple syrup in place of honey
  — substitute sunflower seeds &/or
    nuts for pumpkinseeds
  —add chopped dates or raisins

STORE your crackers, wafers, etc. in airtight containers as with anything you want to keep crisp.

RECRISPING: If <u>any</u> of your beautiful crispies — granola, wafers, chips, whatever — should be left out or improperly stored & lose their crunch, simply return them to your dryer until the old snap comes back. Obviously, this will work with anything that needs crisping, whether your own or a commercial variety.

SESAME~BANANA CRISPS

Couldn't be easier or tastier! We consider this recipe to be a <u>classic</u>.

<u>Blend</u>:
> very ripe bananas with small wedge of lemon

<u>Mix together</u>:
> equal parts puréed bananas & sesame seeds

<u>Spread</u> quite thin (scant ¼") on plastic wrap & dry...
<u>Remove</u> the plastic & finish drying on screen until very crisp, turning once or twice.

VARIATIONS: — a touch of coriander
> — organic orange peel instead of lemon
> — add some pumpkin or sunflower
>   seeds for taste & texture variation

SESAME - SUNFLOWER SQUARES (with APPLE)

The apples give these a nice chewy texture.

<u>Mix together</u>:
> 1 cup apple purée (chopped apples w/skins, &
>   enough water to support blending action)
> ½ cup honey

(if desired, add a little vanilla — or blend a bit of lemon with the apple purée)

<u>Stir in</u>:
> 1½ cups sesame seeds
> 1½ cups sunflower seeds

<u>Spread</u> to ¼" on plastic wrap... When quite dry, remove plastic & turn it over to dry until crisp.

CHIA-FRUIT WAFERS

Super energy!

Soak:

1/2 cup dried apricots in

1 cup water

Blend:

with a few chopped dates, to sweeten (or honey)

Add:

1/4 cup ground chia seeds

Mix together & spread on plastic to dry (about 1/4" thick), as described in General Instructions.

NOTE: Chia or flax seeds can be used to thicken any fruit leather or grain wafer. Use chia seeds in very small amounts, as they thicken quickly.

MILLET WAFERS

Mix together:

1/2 cup ground millet

1 cup raw blender applesauce (as in plain Apple Leather)

pinch of ground rock salt, or sea salt

Spread 1/4" thick on plastic wrap . . . when quite dry, remove plastic & finish drying on screen until thoroughly crisp.

HEALTHY TREATS FOR GRANDCHILDREN*

* . . . of any age!

DATE~NUT CHEWIES

Bound to become one of your favorites. . .

Mix together:

    2 cups Breakfast Cooky base (following page)

    1 cup ground rolled oats, or oat flour

    1/3 cup sunflower seeds, ground

    2 cups chopped dates

    1 cup coarsely-chopped walnuts

Spread onto prepared plastic wrap (see General Instructions), about 1/4" thick.

Dry until firm enough to cut into squares (make them quite small); then dry the squares a little more.

VARIATIONS: — 1 cup of raisins for 1 cup of the dates

           — sunflower seeds instead of nuts

JAMIE'S BREAKFAST COOKIES

So-called because (note the ingredients) they're a meal in themselves.

<u>Blend until smooth</u>:

This is your "cooky base"

- 3/4 cup oil
- 2/3 cup honey
- 3 or 4 large apples, unpeeled, cored & chopped
- 2 tsp. vanilla &/or small wedge organic lemon

<u>Mix in</u>:

- 3 cups rolled oats
- 1 cup sunflower seeds
- 1 cup raisins or chopped dates

<u>Let stand</u> for 1/2 to 1 hour to allow the oats to soak up flavors.

<u>Drop</u> by spoonful onto parchment paper & dry until firm — one or two days, depending on the texture you prefer. (The soft ones should probably be refrigerated, but ours disappear before keeping becomes a problem.)

VARIATIONS: — add 1/2 cup ground flax seed or 1/2 cup sesame seeds
  — add one cup chopped nuts
  — add ground coriander to the cooky base

NOTE: The versatile cooky base, above, makes a delicious & unusual fruit-salad topping. It also tastes great all by itself, pudding-style, with maybe a few chopped nuts or crumbled sesame squares on top. Try it!

APPLE FREEZE   (Laurie's favorite)

Surprise! The cooky base (previous page) freezes into a smooth, delicious "ice cream." If desired, a little cream may be stirred in before freezing to make it even more special.

▶ Freeze in a shallow baking dish — no stirring required!

VARIATION: One night, Apple Freeze came to a potluck all dressed up as a pie, in a simple crust of sesame-seed meal & oil (patted into place before the apple mixture was poured in). The top was garnished with dates & nuts after the filling had set.   (Crust may be easily varied, using ground nuts for part of the sesame-seed meal, etc.)

CAROB FUDGE

We wouldn't eat any other kind.

Mix together: Add:

   1/3 cup honey   1/4 cup carob powder

   1/3 cup water   1 cup ground sunflower seeds

   2 tsp. vanilla   1 cup ground sesame seeds

Work in:

   as many chopped walnuts as the mixture will hold. Pat to 1/2" thick on parchment paper & dry until it holds together, approximately 2 days.   You want it to be chewy.

VARIATION: substitute 1 cup freshly-grated coconut for the sesame meal (we recommend the fresh only).

For NATURAL CITRUS FLAVORS,
always save your organic,* unsprayed
orange & lemon peels. Cut into thin
strips & dry for future use.
▶ To use, simply powder & add to
fruit mixtures, puddings, purées for
leathers — any favorite recipe that
would benefit from the added citrus
tang.

*Never use the peels of <u>non</u>-organically-grown
oranges, which are normally subjected to dyes
which should not be eaten.   Furthermore,
they don't taste as good!   The peels of
naturally-grown oranges & lemons are usually
much sweeter.

HONEYED ORANGE PEEL
An unexpectedly delightful way to use your dried
orange peel.
Simply soak the dried peel in a honey-water
syrup (one part honey to one part water), until
the peel is soft & saturated with the syrup.
Has a tantalizing, tangy-sweet flavor.
May be stored in the refrigerator (use a small
covered jar).

Your dehydrator enables you to produce the best-possible quality dried herbs, with superlative color & flavor.

NOTE: This section is intended primarily to give you some practical information about <u>drying</u> herbs. Our space is too limited to describe individual herbs & their nutritional & medicinal properties. There are some excellent books, including readily-available paperbacks, which do so in detail.*

▶ We suggest that you purchase such an herbal reference (or several) & discover this fascinating field. Almost every weed in your yard is a useful herb... you might start with the lowly dandelion, or maybe some plantain —— even the quack grass. But don't waste them; do it now!

Here is the GENERAL INFORMATION:

Gather each herb "in the season thereof," when it is lush & green, full of chlorophyll. Get in the habit

*Send a stamped, self-addressed envelope if you'd like a list of some of our favorite herbal references.

of carrying a few plastic bags in your pockets when-ever you take a walk.

Avoid picking near roads, where herbs are dusty & subjected to automobile exhaust fumes, etc.

PICK CLEAN. The less "garbage" you gather with your herbs (other plants, twigs, dirt, dead leaves, etc.), the less work for you later.

Rainwashed herbs seldom need additional washing. But ▶ don't pick them dripping wet. Let the sun do some of your work.

Roots need to be scrubbed. If you have a quantity, use your washing machine! First hose off loose dirt, then agitate awhile in a washerful of cold water.

When you've gathered large amounts of herbs, spread them out on old sheets or big towels (keep each kind separate!) in a darkened room to wilt & shrink up a little before loading dehydrator trays. (Herbs left exposed to light will quickly loose their color.) The wilted leaves take less room in the dryer & dry faster, & while they are spread out you have a chance to cull out large stems, dead leaves, etc., before drying.

DRYING
▶ Review General Instructions, in the front of this book.

Arrange herbs loosely on dryer trays, to allow adequate air flow. Rotate trays as advised in General Instructions.

The key to high-quality dried herbs is <u>fast drying</u> at <u>low temperatures</u>. NEVER exceed 105°. Most herbs will dry in one day, & the quality will be excellent.

As herbs dry & shrink, consolidate them, making room for more fresh herbs on the upper trays.

STORING
▶ Make sure your herbs are crackling-dry before packaging. If there is any moisture present, they may be subject to mold & deterioration.

See General Instructions for packaging & storing instructions. Don't forget to <u>label immediately</u>!

Herewith, additional information for some specific herbs:

COMFREY (Symphytum officinale)
If the leaves are very large, as they often are, fold them in half length-wise on a cutting board & slice off the large fleshy center vein & stem. These contain so much moisture they slow down the drying of the leaves (herb quality is best if dried fast). It's wise to

wear gloves to handle the drying leaves if you think
you'll be sensitive to their invisible little prickles.*
Comfrey root must be cut into very small pieces before drying, as it becomes rock-hard & almost
impossible to grind with standard kitchen equipment.
► NEVER attempt to powder it in your blender or
seed grinder.

CHICKWEED (Stellaria media)

We mention chickweed specifically to
include a recipe for chickweed ointment,
a "home remedy" we wouldn't be without.
It seems to work on itches of all kinds — insect bites,
rashes, surface inflammations on any part of the
body.   (Read about chickweed's properties & uses in
your herbal.)
► Gather chickweed when it is most lush & green.
Although easily pulled, it is best cut with scissors or
clippers, to avoid the dirt that comes up with the
roots.   Dry thoroughly & powder.

CHICKWEED OINTMENT:

In a small bowl, mix ¼ cup dried powdered chickweed
with ½ cup home-rendered lard (the commercial kind
contains additives).
Let stand in dehydrator several days, until the lard is

*Applies to borage (Borago officinalis) as well.

very green, having drawn as much as possible from the chickweed.

Strain, & mix in 1 Tbsp. melted beeswax. The "green" lard will have to be heated a bit more to mix easily, but DO NOT OVERHEAT. The beeswax helps solidify the ointment, which otherwise would melt at skin temperature & be very messy. It also has healing properties of its own.

Pour the ointment into small containers & refrigerate what is not in immediate use.

NETTLES (Urtica dioica)

The stinging nettle is such a nutritional boon that everyone should make the effort to gather & dry quantities of them.

Pick with love & gloves. (Latex gloves seem to effectively protect hands from the sting, while allowing freedom of movement.) Even while drying, however, the sting is there; so use gloves for handling throughout the drying process. When dry, crumble the leaves & store in bags as described in General Instructions.

Nettles are incredibly versatile, you'll discover. They make a fine, mild tea — both to drink & to use as a final hair rinse! (They promote a healthy scalp & help prevent graying.) We also add powdered nettles to soups, broths & salads, etc., for nutrition.

USING YOUR HERBS

▶ Refer to your herbal references for specific uses, especially if you are interested in using herbs for healing. Proceed with caution, but don't be afraid to learn!

Even if you are not yet interested in their healing properties, remember that herbs are <u>food,</u> & may be used to enhance your meals every day. And don't forget the simple pleasure of a fragrant cupful of herb tea...

<u>Teas</u> are perhaps the commonest & easiest way to use dried herbs. There is a whole world of herb teas — strong ones, bland ones, minty ones, tangy, bitter & delicate ones. Refreshing, soothing ones. Learn about them!

▶ Generally, use a rounded teaspoonful of dried herb per cup, or more, to taste. (It is not necessary to powder herbs for tea.) Pour boiling water over & steep 5 to 15 minutes. Strain; add a bit of honey if you like. (When using <u>roots</u> or woody stems, simmer for 10 to 20 minutes. But NEVER simmer or boil the leaf.)

Every day we use herbs as <u>food.</u> We always keep several little jars of our favorite freshly-powdered dried herbs on hand (comfrey, dandelion, nettles, malva & chickweed, to name a few) to add a terrific vitamin & mineral boost to almost anything we eat.

MEAT & FISH

The following "recipes" (methods, actually) are pretty classic; you'll find that drying meat & fish is simple & fast.

FISH
(Salmon, halibut, sole, cod, etc.):
Clean & filet. Be sure to remove all fat skin. Dip the cubed fish (½" x 1" is a good size) into soy sauce & dry on a cooky sheet until sufficiently dry to transfer to parchment paper. Dry it quickly; if it will be stored for a long time, dry very hard. If for more or less immediate use, stop the drying at any point desired.
This method gives a delicious, almost smoky flavor.

(Smelt, or other small fish):
Clean, but no need to remove bones. Slit down the middle & lay out flat. Dip into soy sauce, or use the "sprinkle" method: occasionally add soy sauce during drying. (This method is a joy for tasters, because it requires a lot of tasting to get the flavor just right.)
When thoroughly dry, the bones can readily be chewed with the fish. Freshly-dried smelt are

a real treat. Be sure to dry them very hard, however, for long-term storage.

▶ We recommend cool, dark storage in tightly-closed jars for all dried fish or meat.

▶ After drying fish, the dehydrator trays should be thoroughly washed to remove any fishy odor. Setting your dehydrator outside in a protected area such as a carport makes fish drying more pleasant, though really fresh fish are never a problem.

BEEF JERKY
Easy, fast, good results.
Start with <u>very</u> <u>lean</u> meat. Remove all visible fat & slice into thin strips.
(Flank steak is the cut usually used for drying: slice it with the grain for chewiness, or against grain for a more tender jerky.)
Sprinkle meat strips with a little quality salt, if desired. The meat strips dry quickly, taste delicious, with no further ado; but if desired may be dipped into or sprinkled with soy sauce for a different, more "smoky" flavor.
Dry very hard for long-term storage; store in tightly-lidded jars in a cool, dark place.

Try adding bits of jerky to a green salad...

FOWL

Remove any fatty skin or fat tissue. Slice or cut up as desired (keep pieces quite thin, for fast drying). Pieces may be lightly dusted with poultry seasoning before drying, if desired, or with vegetable salt. Dry quickly.

NOVELTY DEPARTMENT: MINCEMEAT LEATHER

For that jar of homemade mincemeat you've been saving.

Purée the mincemeat in your blender & spread evenly over plastic wrap to dry (à la basic Apple Leather), about ¼" thick . . . _voilà_! Mincemeat Leather — unexpected & delicious.

"AFTERTHOUGHTS"

. . . A few more hints, a few more recipes we'd like to share as we go to print again . . . in no particular order, but we hope you'll use & enjoy them.

In the "HINTS" department:

NEVER use <u>wax paper</u> in your dehydrator. We checked our General Instructions (page 3) & see that although we never suggested using it, we didn't say <u>not</u> to, either . . . Some users have found out the hard way that even at the suggested low heat, the wax melts into whatever they're drying.

LABEL fruit leathers <u>as you put them on the trays.</u> Just slip a scrap of paper under the edge of the plastic wrap. Leathers can look so much alike — don't lose the recipe for a really terrific one!

DIP white-meated apples into <u>pineapple juice</u> to keep them white as they dry . . . diluted fresh lemon juice works well, too.

BREAKFAST COOKIES (page 39), we've found, may go directly onto the screens to dry beautifully. Parchment paper is not necessary.

SLICED TOMATOES, also, may be placed directly on screens & dry beautifully. Slice _with_ the stem (vertically), about ¼" thick. They won't drip through screens & just peel off when dry. Thin ones make great "chips."

ONIONS sliced _with_ the stem rather than across it aren't as prone to yellow when they dry, & will dry into beautiful crescent-shapes.

If you DON'T HAVE A BLENDER & want to make fruit leathers: Some fruits may be ground in a food grinder, then pushed through a Foley food mill; soft fruits can also be pushed through a sieve or ricer. Ripe bananas may be mashed with a potato masher. Leathers will have textures slightly different from the puréed kind; all good. Try them even if you do have a blender.

FRUIT LEATHERS can be made from _canned, frozen_ or _soaked dried_ fruits as well as fresh.

GREEN GRAPES, CRANBERRIES, dry in ¼ the time & have nicer color & flavor, if _sliced in half_ instead of drying whole.

Thinly-sliced dried PARSNIPS are crisp & delicious alone or with dips — try them to believe them!

MORE ON USING DRIED FRUITS: SOAKING

Most dried fruits are used "as is," for delicious quick-energy nibbling.   But soaking them adds a new dimension to their versatility.
(See again the recipes on page 23.)

▶ As a rule, plan to soak any dried fruit overnight, for good consistency.   Use plain water; it quickly becomes sweet juice.   <u>Refrigerate</u> what's left ⎯ it ferments quickly at room temperature.

▶ Don't forget to USE THE LIQUID from soaked dried fruits ⎯ for refreshing drinks, or as all or part of the liquid in puddings, shakes, etc.

DRIED BANANAS are deliciously creamy when reconstituted in rich <u>milk.</u> Add a little vanilla & whiz in your blender for banana cream pudding!

Plain soaked dried bananas will make any breakfast <u>eggnog</u> or <u>milkshake</u> rich & creamy. If the bananas are very thin "chips," they may not even require pre-soaking. Try making your shake with <u>juice</u>, as well as the traditional milk.

When your soaked-fruit combination is too tangy, <u>sweeten it naturally</u> by adding bananas, pears, dates...

NEW RECIPE IDEAS

Would you believe dried <u>cottage cheese</u>? We make
our own, & when milk was in great abundance
last year, had more than we could use. So we
dried it, & the results were mouth-watering.

We prefer our own simple & creamy pot-cheese,
but a good commercial variety works as well. A
blender gives it the creamy texture we like, or you
may push it through a sieve. Ricotta cheese is
already smooth & doesn't require puréeing.

<u>MAKE IT SWEET</u>: With Fruit & Honey

<u>The proportions</u>: About half-&-half (one part
cottage cheese to one part puréed fruit), or to
taste, plus honey to sweeten. Add flavorings
(vanilla, spices) as your taste dictates.

<u>The method</u>: Purée the fruit in your blender as
for a fruit leather (see Apple Leather, page 8); add
the cottage cheese & blend smooth. Add honey
to taste & blend. Dry same as Apple Leather...
It's also fun to dry in little leathers, or wafers, about
2"-3" in diameter. Dry to a firm-but-pliable state.

<u>Combinations</u>: Try combining your cottage cheese

with puréed ripe bananas, honey & vanilla (tastes like cheesecake!) —— also delicious with puréed apples — apricots — peaches — berries — or combinations of fruit.   Or, use _no_ fruit: simply combine with honey & vanilla to taste. They're all delicious; you'll think of more.

MAKE IT SAVORY: With Herbs & Seasonings

Method: Same as for Sweet recipes, facing page.

Possibilities: Season the cheese with a favorite seasoning salt — cayenne — garlic powder or crushed fresh garlic — chili powder — etc.

SAVORY TOMATO-CHEESE WAFERS

Blend tomato, cottage cheese & chili powder to taste. You will use more cottage cheese than tomato, as this makes a thinner mixture. Drop by spoonfuls onto tray prepared with plastic wrap as for leather — each spoonful will spread & dry to a nice, pliable wafer.   A delightful hors-d'œuvre or salad accompaniment.   Good way to use leftover stewed or canned tomatoes or tomato paste.

NOTE: Cottage cheese may be dried plain & soaked back to soft consistency for later use. Texture will be slightly different. Good for cooking uses.

YOUR OWN POT CHEESE:
Delicious, creamy & a little different each time
you make it.

This method works with any milk; we like to use
our own creamy goat milk, raw & fresh. You
may use skim or whole milk, raw or pasteurized.

► It is the straining that gives the cheese its
quality. Nylon organdy is perfect for this purpose:
its density is ideal, it washes easily (you can towel
it dry), & it lasts indefinitely. A 20" x 20" square
is enough.
[We have a friend who strains his cheese with coffee
filter papers in a funnel & says it works great.]

In a large stainless steel pan, put 3 quarts of the
milk of your choice. You may use it straight from
the refrigerator or gently warm it on the stove.
Add ½ cup of good buttermilk, your own or a
commercial variety. You may scrape a few
grains off a tablet of rennet into the milk.*

* Rennet is not necessary & we don't use it, ourselves.
It does speed up the process somewhat, but tends
to make the watching more critical: once past
the "turning point," when you can see the curd & whey
begin to separate, the cheese begins to get grainy.

Place the covered pan atop your dehydrator, in back near the ventilation opening, or in any consistently warm place (about 100°). Let it stand until a firm curd is formed — it may take anywhere from 12 to 24 hours, or even longer. It varies a lot, so don't worry if it seems to be taking a long time.

Line a collander with the nylon organdy & set it over a large pan. Carefully dip the thick milk into the lined collander. (If you pour it reck-lessly, it may run right through your strainer.) ►The consistency of the milk at this point may range from that of thick buttermilk to a firmer curd. It doesn't seem to matter as long as it's thick enough to stay in the collander. Allow it to drain overnight or longer. To finish the draining, pick up the edges of the organdy to form a "bag" of cheese & devise a way to hang it so that more whey can squeeze out (we twist it around a hook we put in just for that purpose). Avoid twist-ing or squeezing the bag itself — you'll just squeeze out the cheese. Let it drain a few more hours.

The result is a superior soft cottage cheese with a tart cream-cheese sort of flavor. Use it in many ways, from dips to dressings. Mixed with honey & vanilla, it once topped a wedding cake deliciously!

"ON THE TRAIL"

Most of the recipes featured in this
book are ideal trail food: lightweight, nutritious &
tasty, they fulfill the prime requirements of hikers
& backpackers. The following ideas are especially
good for this purpose:

DRIED SOUP

Nothing can beat your own delicious soup for
flavor & nutrition. Dry it! Thick, homemade
legume soups — bean, split pea, lentil — are
perfect for drying. A good canned soup works, too.

<u>The method</u>: Briefly purée your thick bean soup,
in blender, electric mixer, or with potato masher,
until it has a fairly smooth consistency.
<u>Dry</u> same as Apple Leather, page 8, except in 2"-
3" wafers (drop from a spoon & spread to uni-
form ¼" – ½" thickness).

<u>To use</u>: The dried wafers are excellent just as
they are. For a hot, delicious instant soup,
drop a few wafers into cup or bowl & cover with
boiling water. Steep, stir & enjoy!

▶ Don't forget that classic, powdered Vegetable
Broth, page 28.

<u>More trail food</u>:

CHICKEN OR TURKEY LEATHER
Just as good for at-home munching.

Carefully remove bones from leftover cooked chicken or turkey. Avoid using very fatty pieces, which make the leather too greasy.
Put the bits & pieces of meat into blender, with enough liquid (chicken stock, broth, & /or water) to blend. (A meat grinder may be used.)
Be sure to add any leftover dressing!
<u>Season</u> to your liking: poultry seasoning; garlic or celery salt; cayenne; perhaps a touch of lemon juice or vinegar. Don't over-season — it gets a bit stronger as it dries.
<u>Dry</u> as for Apple Leather, page 8, on trays prepared with plastic wrap.
Cut into squares, or simply tear off pieces to eat.

▶ For another way to dry fowl, see the recipe on page 50.

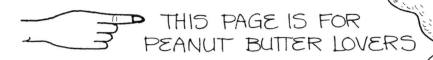 THIS PAGE IS FOR
PEANUT BUTTER LOVERS

Peanut butter added to fruit leathers
makes a real confection!   Try these:

APPLE- PEANUTBUTTER LEATHER
Prepare 4 cups chopped apples (cored
but not peeled) as for basic Apple Leather,
page 8.
To the puréed apples, add one cup old-
fashioned peanut butter, & honey to taste
(honey is optional).   Blend together & dry
same as basic Apple Leather.

BANANA - PEANUTBUTTER LEATHER
<u>Purée in blender</u>:
     3 cups ripe (soft) bananas
<u>Add</u>: 1 cup old-fashioned peanut butter
     1 tsp. vanilla
<u>Blend</u> all together, spread onto prepared trays
& dry as above.

VARIATIONS:
Add 1 heaping tablespoon carob powder for a
rich, chocolate-y taste.
Stir in ½ cup chopped walnuts.

LIVING FOODS DEHYDRATOR

PARTS LIST
DIRECTIONS FOR CONSTRUCTION
DRAWINGS

PARTS LIST

DEHYDRATOR CABINET & TRAYS

2	Side panels	24" x 19¼"	⎫
1	Back panel	23" x 19¼"	⎬ ½ sheet
1	Front panel	24" x 4"	⎪ ½" plywood
1	Door	24" x 14¾"	⎭
4	Legs	1½" x 1½" x 22"	
1	Lid	22¾" x 23⅜" (Masonite)	
16	Tracks	¾" x ¾" x 22¹⁵⁄₁₆"	
2	Front & back upper braces	¾" x 1½" x 21½"	
24	Tray frame sides	¾" x ¾" x 22½"	

(for six trays)

(Legs, tracks, braces, frame sides — fir, pine, or hemlock)

24	Wood strips	⅛" x ¾" x 22" (paneling)	
12'	Screening	(see cutting instructions — Screening #1)	

HARDWARE

2	Cabinet hinges
2	Flexa Door Catch
1	Wood knob 1¼" diameter
1	Elmer's Glue-All
12	Flat Head Wood Screws 1½" x #10, w/ finish washers (legs)
12	Finish nails (6 D) 2" (upper braces)

100	Nails	1" (tracks & WAG supports)
25	Finish nails (4 D)	1½" (panels)
¼ lb.	Nails	½" or ⅝" (tray frame corners/ strips)

HEATER   See SPECIAL NOTES

| 1 | "WAG" (Warm Air Generator) |
| 2 | WAG supports ¾" x ¾" x 12" |

TOOLS NEEDED

Hammer
Screwdriver
Staple gun (optional)
Drill
Exacto knife, sharp knife, or razor-edged tool
Ruler
Sandpaper for finishing

DEHYDRATOR CABINET ASSEMBLY

Match the panels for appearance & direction of face grain, marking right & left front & back on the inside surfaces.

TRACKS

On the inside surface of the left side panel, lay out the positions of the tracks (Dwg. 1 & 2A). Note that the ends of the tracks <u>must</u> be at least 9/16" from the back & 1/2" from the front edges of the side panel. Start the first track 1/4" from top of side panel and work downward, measure 1 7/8" between lower edges of each track. Attach the tracks with glue & 1" nails, about 5 (five) nails per track. Reverse for right side panel.

DOOR, FRONT & BACK PANELS

Assemble door & front panel by marking the hinge locations & tapping the screw holes with a nail. Be sure that the hinge pins are centered & aligned properly, so that the door will open straight (Dwg. 4A).

Attach WAG supports to the insides of the front & back panels, centering them at the very bottom edges, using glue & 1" nails (Dwg. 2A & 2B).

PANELS

Attach the side panels to the back panel with 5 (five) 1½" finish nails. (Please carefully note placement of panels as shown in Dwg. 3.) Drive nails through the side panel into the _edge_ of the _back_ panel.

Attach front panel (below door) to side panels with 1½" finish nails (Dwg. 4A). (Again, note position in Dwg. 3.) Door is ¼" lower than side panels to allow lid to slide forward for ventilation (Dwg. 4A). Drive nails through front panel into _edge_ of _side_ panels.

FRONT & BACK BRACES

Install the upper front brace between the top tracks (Dwg. 2A & 3), flush with the front edge of tracks. Install the upper back brace between the top tracks (Dwg. 3), four inches forward from back panel. Using 2" finish nails, predrill & drive nails (two to each end of each brace) through side panel, through top track, into end of brace.

LEGS

Legs can be tapered on two adjoining sides if

desired. Attach legs into corners of cabinet, abutting bottom track (untapered sides facing into corners) (Dwg. 2A). Use 1½" x #10 flat head wood screws with cup finish washers, three for each leg (two on the sides, one on the front/back) (Dwg. 4A & 4B). Predrill, being sure to avoid the nails attaching panels together (Dwg. 4A).

DOOR CATCH & KNOB

Mount a "Flexa Door Catch" on the inside surface of the third track from the bottom (set in ⅛" from end of track) (Dwg. 2A) — one catch on each side.

Insert the screw part of the latch into the receiver, leaving the point sticking out. Shut the door so that the screw point marks the inside surface of the door panel. Mount the screws at these points. Adjust length of screw by screwing in or out.

Install the knob on the door face (Dwg. 4A).

LID

The lid is not attached to the dehydrator but is simply laid into the recessed top. It slides forward to create the necessary ventilation opening (two inches, maximum). See Page 1, Ventilation.

TRAY ASSEMBLY

Frame. Sand tray frames to be sure they are smooth for future ease of cleaning. Assemble tray frames, using glue & ½" or 5/8" nails (Dwg. 5A).

Screening. After trays are nailed together to form frame, install screening as follows:

1. Cut each tray screen larger than frame by at least 1".

2. Place frame on a flat surface & apply a bead of glue on two adjoining sides of frame.

3. Lay screen tautly on frame, aligning the edge of the screen with the glued sides of the tray. (The screen should overhang only on the unglued sides.)

4. Lay wood strips over the glued sides so that they cover the joints in the frame (Dwg. 5B). This adds strength to the finished tray. Nail with ½" or 5/8" nails. Be generous with nails.

5. Allow the glue to dry overnight. Once the glue has dried, the screen may be pulled tightly as the remaining two sides are attached.

6. Apply a bead of glue over the screen to the remaining two sides. Starting at one end of a side, stretch screen tautly & nail. Do the same at the opposite end of the last side. The other nails can then be placed, stretching & firming the screen as you work.

   It is extremely important that screens be as tight as possible. An available tool such as an artist's canvas stretcher, or an extra pair of hands to stretch & hold the screen while you nail, would be invaluable.

7. Let glue dry completely & trim excess screen. Any rough edges of tray may be sanded for ease of handling.

   (Trays are reversible, but most people use them with tray frame up for efficient food placement.)

OPTIONAL

THE SEVENTH TRAY

Materials not included in parts list.

HEAVY-DUTY TRAY

If you desire, you may order or construct a heavy-duty tray, using ¼" hardware cloth.* Construct the standard tray frame. Add three evenly spaced braces, ¾" x ¾" x 21⅜". (See dwg. below.) Nail these braces to frame, using 1½" finish nails (predrill).

* Square-cut the hardware cloth to an accurate 22½" x 22½", using wire cutters. This material cannot be stretched or glued, but otherwise the mounting procedure is identical with the screen construction.

braces

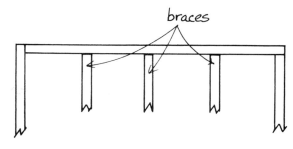

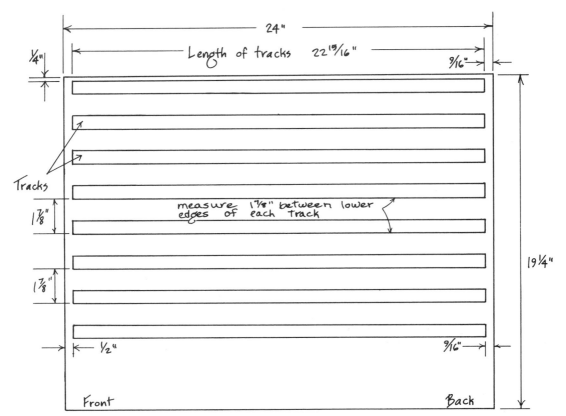

24"

Length of tracks   22¹⁹⁄₁₆"

¼"

⁹⁄₁₆"

Tracks

measure 1⅞" between lower
edges of each Track

1⅞"

19¼"

1⅞"

½"

⁹⁄₁₆"

Front

Back

Left side panel.   Label inside
of each panel, "front," "back,"
"left side," "right side."

DWG. #1.
Inside view of left side panel.
(Reverse for right side.)

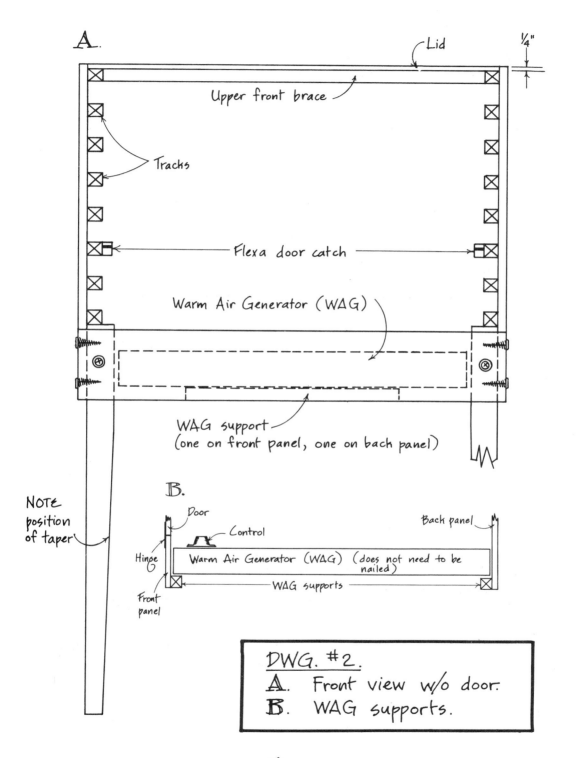

A.

Lid

¼"

Upper front brace

Tracks

Flexa door catch

Warm Air Generator (WAG)

WAG support
(one on front panel, one on back panel)

NOTE
position
of taper

B.

Door

Control

Back panel

Hinge

Warm Air Generator (WAG) (does not need to be nailed)

Front
panel

WAG supports

DWG. #2.
A. Front view w/o door.
B. WAG supports.

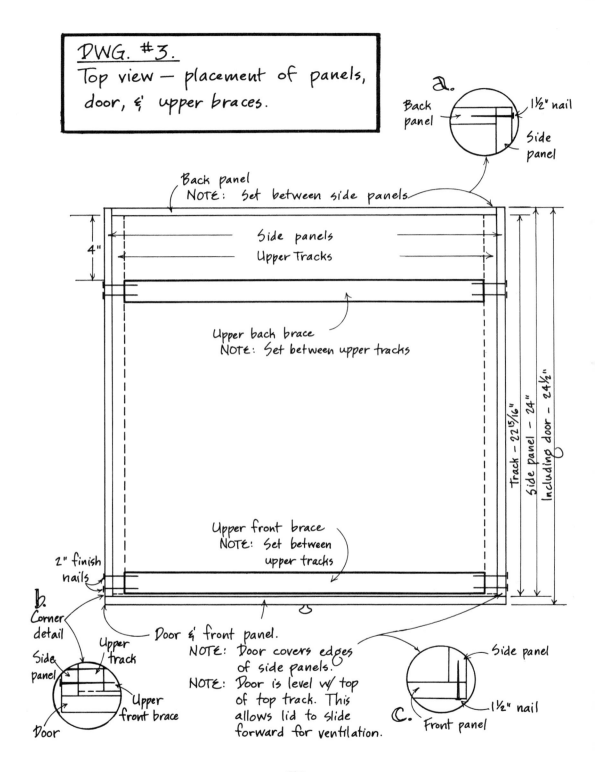

DWG. #3.
Top view — placement of panels, door, & upper braces.

a.

Back panel

1½" nail

Side panel

Back panel
NOTE: Set between side panels.

4"

Side panels
Upper Tracks

Upper back brace
NOTE: Set between upper tracks

Track – 22¹⁵/₁₆"

Side panel – 24"

Including door – 24½"

Upper front brace
NOTE: Set between upper tracks

2" finish nails

b.
Corner detail

Side panel

Upper track

Upper front brace

Door

Door & front panel.
NOTE: Door covers edges of side panels.
NOTE: Door is level w/ top of top track. This allows lid to slide forward for ventilation.

Side panel

1½" nail

c.
Front panel

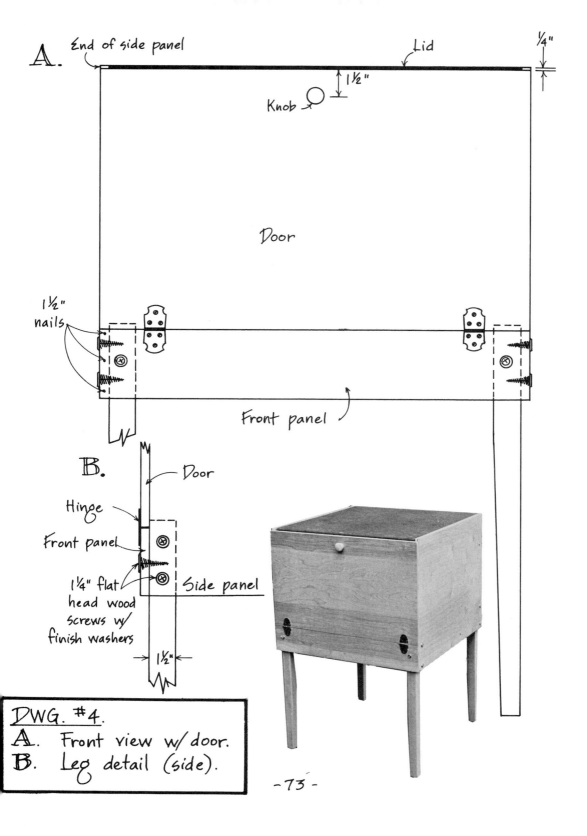

A. End of side panel

Lid

¼"

1½"

Knob

Door

1½" nails

Front panel

B.

Door

Hinge

Front panel

1¼" flat head wood screws w/ finish washers

Side panel

1½"

DWG. #4.
A. Front view w/ door.
B. Leg detail (side).

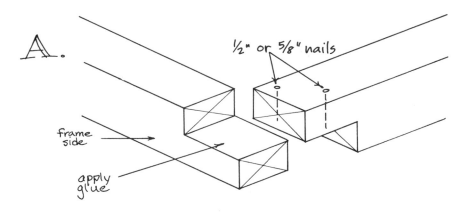

A.

½" or ⅝" nails

frame
side

apply
glue

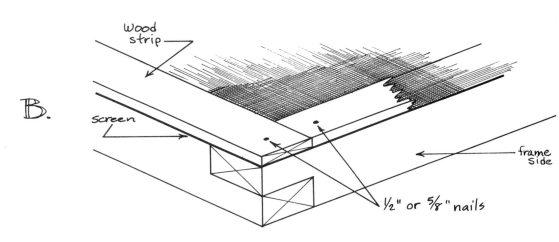

B.

wood
strip

screen

frame
side

½" or ⅝" nails

DWG. #5. Tray Frame Detail.
A. Lap joint.
B. Wood strip & screen.

SPECIAL NOTES

HEATER

An efficient low-heat unit (100° - 110°) ideal for this dehydrator is the Warm Air Generator ("WAG"), designed & manufactured by Living Foods Dehydrators (Box 546, Fall City WA 98024). Other possibilities, some of them temporary, include:

- A hot water radiator under the dehydrator;
- A low-wattage (less than 2000) oven or clothes-dryer element adapted to 120V;
- A wall heater w/ thermostat, 1200W, 120V;
- An open waffle iron, hot plate, or electric frypan w/ variable control.

▶ Remember that electrical requirements must be carefully noted & all safety measures taken.

OPERATION

Although we have successfully used & recommended a thermostatically controlled wall-type heater with circulating fan, in fact neither thermostat nor fan is necessary. The primary considerations are that heat be LOW (100° - 110°) and that the air CIRCULATE FREELY. The bottom of our dehydrator is open so that air can enter through & around the heater. A gentle current is created as the warmed air naturally rises toward the opening at the top, in a chimney effect. No fan is required. The moving air dries food quickly, with no mildew, because it takes the moisture with it.

A two-inch ventilation opening is maximum for greatest drying efficiency. When the dehydrator is not in use, the lid may be closed to keep the interior dust-free.

THE FIRST OF MANY IS STILL THE BEST OF ALL

Years ago when we built our first dehydrator, there were no others on the market. Although there are many to choose from today, ours remains unique in its versatility, functional design and efficiency.

CHECK THESE FEATURES

VERSATILE DESIGN
The Living Foods Dehydrator, with its low temperature settings and roomy design, can be used for a variety of purposes, including home-made pasta and breads, seeds and sprouts, and of course, fruits, vegetables and herbs.

ENERGY EFFICIENT
The Living Foods Dehydrator does not require a fan for its efficient drying. The top ventilated dryer creates a "chimney" effect; as air enters through the screened heater at the bottom, it warms and rises, taking moisture with it out the top. This unique use of heat convection eliminates noisy and costly fans, reduces energy consumption and makes it easy to convert from electricity to alternate heat sources.

LARGE CAPACITY
The Living Foods Dehydrator provides more drying space for your dollar than any other dehydrator on the market.

BUILT TO LAST

• THE CABINET
The cabinet is solidly crafted from half-inch interior quality plywood. The hinged door drops down 180° when open and is completely out of the way when loading or removing trays.

• THE HEATER
The heater is our specially designed Warm Air Generator (WAG). Its infinite thermostatic control is adjustable and provides an even, constant heat (between 80° and 130°). Created specifically for the low temperature requirements of food dehydration, the WAG can operate 24 hours a day safely and efficiently.

• THE TRAYS AND SCREENING
We are proud to offer a screen that is absolutely food safe. It is made of heat-fused polypropylene which does not stretch with use. It provides a tough non-stick surface and is easy to clean. Our screen is not available in retail outlets.

Note: Utility and window screening is not suitable for food dehydration due to harmful chemicals used in the manufacturing process.

DO-IT-YOURSELF
• The Living Foods Dehydrator is a perfect do-it-yourself project. We offer kits, parts and plans.

CALL OR WRITE
Living Foods Dehydrators
3023-362nd Avenue S.E., Fall City, Washington 98024 (425) 222-5587